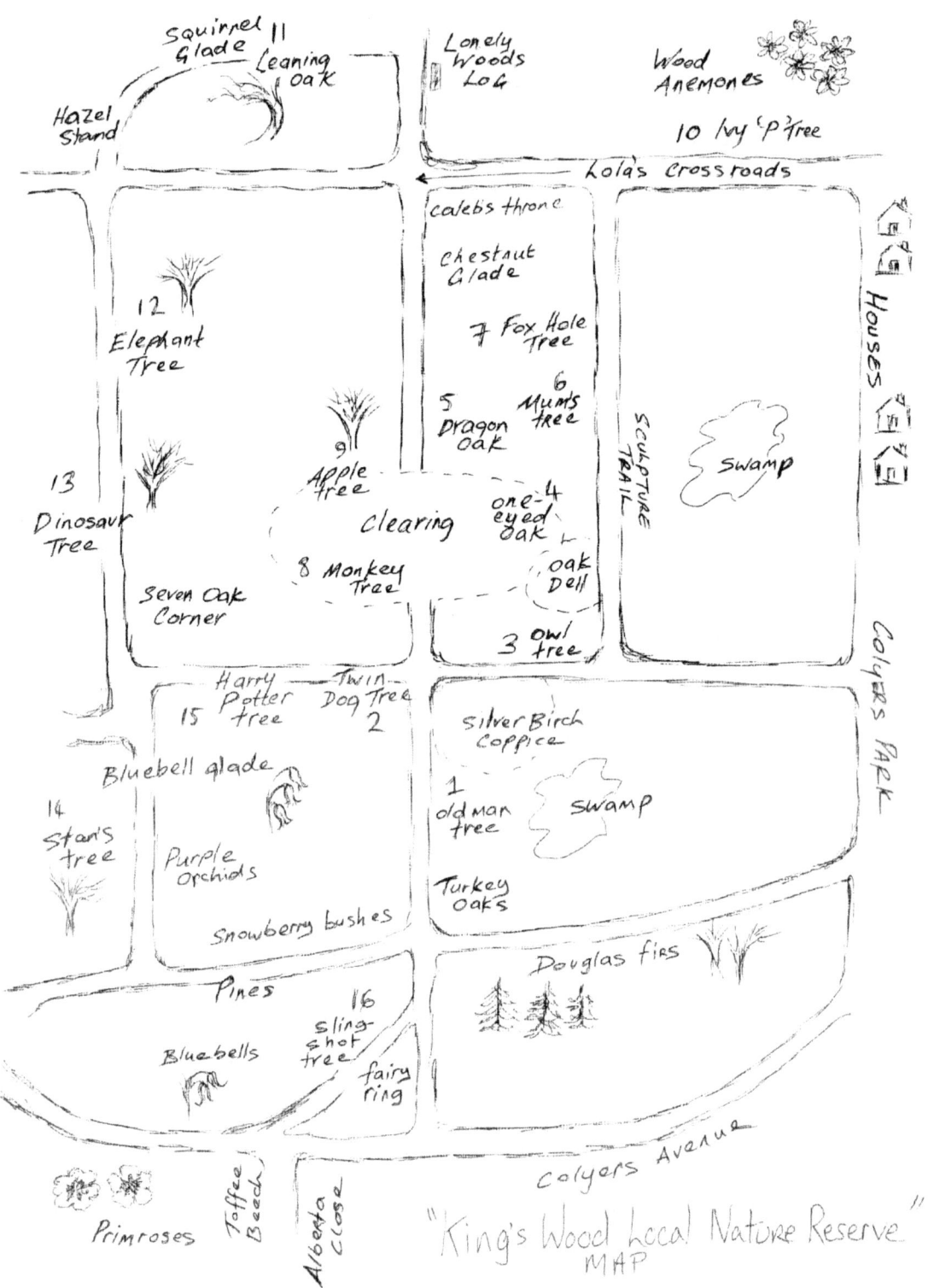

Impressions
of an
English Woodland

Illustrated Edition

Also by Paula Boulton:

Women of Steel: A Living History of Corby
First edition - Corby Zone 2008
Second edition - CompletelyNovel 2018

Forthcoming:
Shouting for 20 Years
(Compendium of plays written for Shout! Youth Theatre)
Lunarlink Publishing Collective

Lunarlink Publishing Collective

Impressions of an English Woodland

My year in Kingswood

Paula Boulton

Illustrations by Fanoulla Georgiou

First published in UK in 2020
by Lunarlink Publishing Collective
43 Epsom Walk, Corby, Northants
NN189JJ

ISBN 9781787234826

Words and music copyright © Paula Boulton 2020
Illustrations © Fanoulla Georgiou
Cover photos © Kate Dyer
Bluebell insert © Lorraine Maria Dziarkowska

All rights reserved. No part of this publication may be reproduced, stored in a retrieval system, or transmitted, in any form or by any means (electronic, mechanical, photocopying, recording or otherwise), without the prior permission of the publisher.

Typeset in Palatino Linotype
Book layout and design by Spider Redgold
Cover design by Malgorzata Nikodem

Lunarlink Publishing
Collective

*To Julie, my poetry-loving big sister,
who, like me, knows every inch of our glorious Kingswood*

About the book

In 2016 I accepted the commission of a lifetime. I was asked to create new work based on my relationship with Kingswood, a remnant of the ancient Rockingham Forest five minutes stroll from my flat. At the end of the process I was to invite the public to join me for a walk.

The "Our Woods" brochure stated:

"Paula will take you off the beaten track to some of the places which have inspired her musical compositions and poems. The walk will include performances of her work."

All this was to celebrate the urban woodlands of Corby, my home town, and to engage and involve people in enjoying and learning about them.

Between April 2016 and April 2017 I made regular trips to Kingswood, which has always been my outdoor studio anyway. It became an intimate part of my daily thinking and observation and to record that journey was a joy. Some days it was words which flowed, capturing the sights, the sounds, the feel of the place. Other days I would be riveted by some birdsong and a musical idea would emerge. You will find these notated throughout the book.

The return of spring after a year of such close encounters seemed truly miraculous and I had the joy of leading sixty people around Kingswood to share the moment. Dressed as the Woman of the Woods and accompanied by sixteen members of my new orchestra and four violin pupils, I read and played extracts from my new work in a truly magical happening.

Following requests from participants to make the writing available, I have finally done so. I sincerely hope it will allow you to experience this beautiful corner of England's green and pleasant land.

If ever you are passing - stop off for a stroll! I promise you it will be worth it.

Paula Boulton May 23rd 2020 Corby

Foreword

I first met Paula Boulton in 2019 in beautiful Snowdonia, Wales. As we hiked the Panorama Walk near Barmouth, we found we were kindred spirits, sharing a deep love of Nature and of poetry.

Later, when Paula asked if I would help edit a book of poems she had been commissioned to write about the ancient woodlands close to her home in Corby, Northamptonshire, I was delighted. She told me that The King's Wood, once the royal hunting forest of Rockingham, was a protected local nature reserve, easily accessible to residents of the nearby Kingswood housing estate and to the local schoolchildren.

For those of us without gardens or easy access to parks and green spaces, Paula's Impressions of an English Woodland can take us directly into a place of peace and tranquillity, and remind us of the everyday joys of connecting with Nature. We enjoy meeting the trees, animals and people Paula encounters in this woodland, and we come to share an appreciation of it.

As I write, the Covid-19 lockdown is still in place in Wales, and all across the country people have been staying home and trying to protect themselves and others from the virus. Opportunities to get out into the countryside and enjoy the beauties of spring are impossible for some and limited for many; these poems help to bring Nature to us, wherever we are. Paula's voice, gentle and humorous, curious and reflective, is ever alive to the beauty of the woods. We too can hear the bluebells calling, be entranced by 'beckoning primroses', and see the colours change with the seasons in this 'overgrown green paradise'.

Impressions of an English Woodland offers us some sanctuary and joy in these difficult times, and beyond. Let Paula's unique way of seeing take you on a 'tread-lightly' journey of a year in Kingswood. It will do your soul good.

May 2020
Bronwen Evans
Ceredigion, Wales

Poems

April
Bluebells Calling — 3
Primroses — 7
Primrose in G — 8

May
The Greening — 12
Born in the Time of Bluebells — 13
Sightings — 15
Ancient and Modern — 16
Night Song — 18
Dinosaur — 19
Tent 1 — 20
Tent 2 — 21
Fallen — 23

June
The Insects Prevail — 26
On Dog Walkers — 28
The Glow Worm — 30
Footprints — 31

July
Woodland Deprivation Syndrome — 34

August
Goodbye to the Woods — 39

September
End of Summer — 42
Autumn Glimpse — 42
Stewardship — 43
Autumn Nights — 44
Tortoise Pace — 46
Fecund — 51

October
The Sky is Falling — 55
Coppice — 56
Dog Tree — 57
A Haunt of Peace — 58
The World Turned Upside Down — 60
Colour Box — 61
Artists — 61

Going Bald	61
Abscission	63

November
Room to Breathe	67
Who's First?	68
Tinsel	69
Treetop Land	71
Impressions	74
From Above	74
Tree Orchestra	75
Late Autumn 1	76
Late Autumn 2	77

December
Betwixt and Between	80
The Photo Time Machine	81
Space	82
Oak Abscission Day	84
Three Leaves	86
Five Leaves and an Immigrant Dog	88
Air, Land or Sea	90

January
Winter walk 1	94
Winter walk 2	95
Bare Trees	97
The Squirrel	97

February
Pathways	100
Waiting	100
The Stirring	101
Storm Doris	101

March
Moonstruck	104
Peter and the Wolf	105
The Quickening	106
Persephone's Return	108

April
The Bees are Dying	113
The Joy of Living	114

Sketches

King's Wood Local Nature Reserve MAP	ii, 121
Magnolia	1, 111
Bluebells	11
Abseiling Spider	25
Tunnel of Trees	33
Cascading Overgrowth	37
Apples and Blackberries	41
Squirrel	53
Acorns	65
Oak Leaf	79
Bare Branch	93
Snow Drop	99
Primroses	103

Music Scores, Rhythms and Snippets

Song Fragment	2
Drones in G	9
Birdcall	14
Cuckoo and Birdcalls	14
Transcribed from Phone	17
Blackbird - Transcribed from Phone	19
Left Right Caw	35
Red Kite	38
Wood Pigeon	38
Stepping in the Woods	50
Rhythm l	57
Birdcall	70
Rhythm ll	70
Birdcall Dvôrak	73
Rhythm lll	89
Birdcall (Peter and the Wolf)	105
Birdcall and Rhythm	107
Teacher teacher birdcall	107
Birdbop string melody	109
Score of Amazon Echo from Forest Fragments	116
Score of Birdbop from Forest Fragments	117

12th April
Bluebells Calling

On waking the bluebells called to me
"We're here!
Come and find us"
Donning my walking-in-the-woods apparel
I hastened to the King's Wood
Images of wood anemones, orchids, wild garlic, celandine and yes, bluebells
Emblazoned on my inner eye

I had seen some the day before
Strewn across a south-facing bank in Ilam Park
A delightful surprise
Visceral excitement
If they had bloomed already in the frozen North
Where two weeks previously I had climbed in six inches of snow
Surely in the season-muddled south they would also have emerged?

And so I go!

Slipping my feet into mud-encrusted wellies
I reflect on how I feel back here in the wet and mud and green
Nearly two weeks in the Spanish desert had almost dried up my soul
Which yearned for green, for moist, for wet

First sight of England's green patchwork
Through the window of the plane
Always enthrals me
Tells me I am home

The writing of this short paragraph as I walk
Is the distance from my doorway to green

And here I stand
Listening to the cacophony of birdsong
Drawn to the beckoning ring of primroses
And more - bluebells, daisies, celandines, dandelions

The entry way into the Woods is lined with bluebells
Sticky burs
Strangely tall and overgrown grasses reach high, tall and straight
Etiolation
Violets, waxy medieval lords and ladies
Clumps and clusters of leaves - some pitted with pock marks
Buds unfurling, poking through

At the swamp, two ducks swim serenely through the green plankton
Writing appears as the green gives way in their wake
Contrails in the water
They stop, and momentarily they are plaster ducks in a garden

I am reminded of Peter and the Wolf
Da duh de duh
I almost expect the Wolf to appear as they waddle to the bank
Duh de duh
Here's the cat, and the bird flies up into the tree
"Look out" cries Peter -
but it is too late
The oboe-squawking duck disappears after a frantic chase around the swamp

But this duck stands its ground
Beautiful iridescent green head-feathers
Remind me of recently seen peacocks in Spain
What stunning colours nature gives to the birds

I gaze upon a sea of bluebells
The shimmering blue invites me to another world
An orchid appears before me
Wild strawberries
Multiple shades of green, impossible to count
Life burgeoning despite or due to so much rain

For a moment the seasons collide
New buds fight through leaf mulch and last year's dying brambles
The tangle and turmoil twisting and turning
The greening begins on the ground
First the carpet
Then moss creeping up trunks
Leaves appearing slowly on bushes and shrubs
And a smattering of green above
Where mostly there are still stark bare branches
Though hawthorn blossom powders some trees with white

Uniquely formed spindly hazel trees
Lead me to admire other curling trunks
Fascinating shapes
Our very own sculpture park

Thick sticky buds announce to me an errant chestnut tree
New, very thin - but ready to burst

Unusual thick rope-like striations
Diagonally wrapped around a new hazel tree
Draw my eye to rusty lichen

Opposite - I see that my wood anemones are back
Same patch, same place
They sleep soundly
Quietly, I tiptoe towards them
Not wishing to disturb

Such a huge, vibrant energy field
Why here I wonder?
Is it the sun that wakes them up
Invites them to stretch out, open up
And drink the sunlight?

Stepping over the crossroads
The dominant visual becomes the white paint lichen
It is competing with thick moss to cover the trunks
I take a new path
It leads to the Elephant Tree
Incredible variegated mosses
Only small sporadic patches of flowers and colours
This could be a different wood

And then my eye is caught by the familiar vast carpet of blue up ahead
The same area each year
Like a kid in a sweet shop I can't get enough
I take a picture and send it to my friend Kate - a yearly ritual
The botanist in me wonders what combination of light, shade
pH, acidity
Causes the bluebells to flourish here

Raw tree innards catch my eye
A trunk has split as a large limb has fallen
The ripped fabric rent asunder reveals the inner flesh of the tree
Strangely intimate - a wound or gash

Splodging my way out of the Woods
Smiling at such simple pleasures
I give thanks again for the joy of living next to this wooded wonderland
This cauldron, where nature brews her ancient miracles

22nd April
Primroses

Not for me the manicured perfection of the tended garden
I prefer the profusion of patches of proliferating primroses
Shivering in their innocent yellow sleeveless poplin dresses

There is a presencing with Primroses
An is-ness
Is that a word?
It should be
There they sit, complete in their basket
Impossible to ignore
Quietly demanding attention

Come closer - witness our perfection

But it is the colour more than anything else
Which takes me back to the innocence of girlhood
For primroses are definitely female

Where do they go when they are gone?

27th April
Primrose in G

The presencing of patches of proliferating primroses holds me spellbound
Such simple beauty and vulnerability
Nestled amongst the yellow ones are two pink ones with yellow centres
They seem out of place but they hold their own

Here I sit - encircled - unable to look away
Head slowly turning in a clockwise ellipse

This stillness is an illusion
They seem not to move
Yet the imperceptible growth
The opening and closing of petals to greet the sun
Surely that constitutes movement?
And they shiver in the breeze
They are moved

But essentially they claim their spot on the earth and be
Resilient and returning despite grass cutters and trampling feet
Their fundamental frequency is a consistent low hum
The note G I think
Interestingly the key of my Bird Bop piece
In the Forest Fragment Suite I am composing

Yesterday I sat amongst bluebells
Sought wood anemones
Greeted primroses and violets

So intent was I on looking at the forest floor I forgot to look up
Today I lift my gaze

The mid-layer is filling quickly with hazel and hawthorn
But far above
Although they were the last to shed
The oaks are getting dressed

Not the turkey oak as yet
But most of the common oaks have donned a light vest of green
The bare ash seem dead
It is tempting to keep my eyes on the ground
But there is mystery in the return of the tree coverings

Are they too fooled by the exceptionally warm weather?
How will they fare in the predicted cold spell?
I resolve to go and gaze upon the month-early cherry blossoms
Before I leave for three days in the Peak District
Where spring may not yet have sprung and can be experienced all over again

The joy of a country with regional weather
Where I can replay the seasons

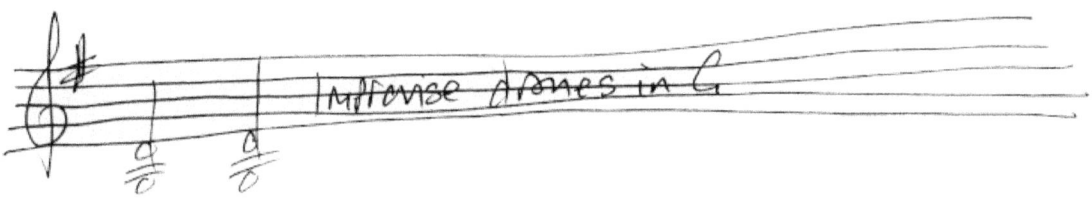

2nd May
The Greening

The greening begins from the ground up
Like sap rising
Green mercury in a thermometer
Spreading up the trunks
Ground cover complete, the canopy is filling out
At bush level a tangle of small-leaved hawthorn are spreading their wings
Creepers are creeping
Chestnut leaves hang limpid like a seven-pronged umbrella
"Oak before the Ash"
Portent of a dry summer
Is turning some treetops the yellow-green of oak blossom
Showing me how many ancient oaks live in these woods

4th May
Born in the Time of Bluebells

Thirsty for bluebells I head for the Woods
Pondering on whether BDS is a real condition
Bluebell Deprivation Syndrome

Knowing that they are there - so close
A five-minute stroll away
Forces me to pay attention

To gaze upon
Sit amongst
Commune with
Imbibe the energy of this simple woodland flower
Feels like an absolute HAVE TO in a pile of shifting priorities

They quietly request my presence
On this first day of your life
But the command is heard and understood deep in my core

Theirs is a short life
May yours be long

If I ignore their compelling presence
I will miss the sight and have to wait until next spring
To bathe in this deep blue glory

And so I sit and fulfil my soul's purpose
Witness to the beauty of blue against green
In a sunlit glade spotted with yellow stars
Amongst the tall trees
In this wild garden of mine
This King's wood

Welcome Reye Scarlett* - a beautiful time to be born

---

*Written for my great-niece Reye Scarlett the day she was born, and read at her christening

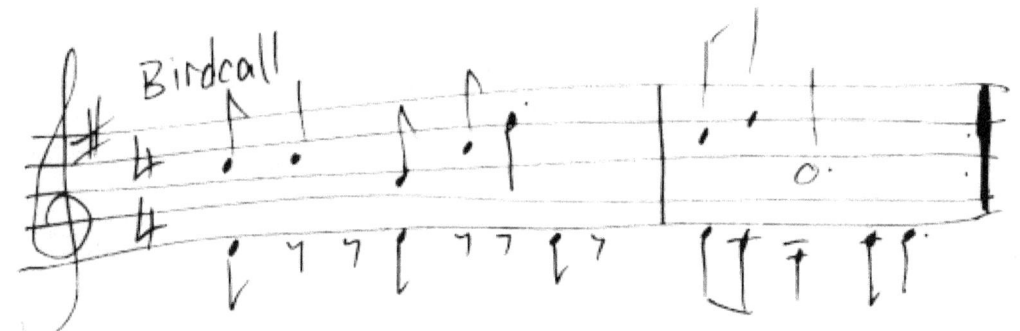

10th May
Sightings

After heavy rain I run to the Woods to see the effect
White campion greet me on the way into the Woods
Tightly-furled ferns getting ready to unfurl
Apple blossom
Sadly it is already time to say goodbye to the fading bluebells
The nettles are on the rise beginning to eclipse them
And pink Herb Robert are mixed in now with the blue
I thank them for their beauty and go on my way

I find the orchids in their usual place

The greening has continued apace
One tree looks half painted
The last to green seem to be the ash
Maple and sycamore come through unnoticed
I notice lilac too and lovely long-haired birch
Candles on the chestnut trees are almost ready
What a journey from sticky buds to magnificent candle
The cherry blossom hangs on for dear life after last night's heavy downpour

All too soon it will be gone

Botanical notes:

Herb Robert: pink flowers, fern-shaped leaves
Greater stitchwort: star-shaped white flowers with ten petals
Sorrel: white flower with five petals, leaves resemble wild strawberry, clustered like a shamrock

12th May

Ancient and Modern

Felt compelled to visit the Woods at nine o'clock as night fell
The birds were "singing in" the night
Fascinated, I recorded their evensong
Intent on comparing it to the morning chorus

And all at once it stopped
With one accord they had fallen silent
What was the signal?

At what point does the fading light of day
Become the approaching dark of night?
At what precise moment does a day end?
Are the birds now tucked up in bed
Snuggled in their nests
Getting some shut eye before their next concert?
In the sudden stillness, a new sound is heard

The whispering of the leaves as the wind gathers speed
And treetops billow and swirl making random beautiful circles in the sky

I gaze upwards and see thick puffy pillows of oak leaves
Dominating the sky line
Reaching into the airspace of the (only-just-out) ash canopy

Who wins in the battle for light?
Soon the entire canopy will close over
And the forest floor will have months to wait
Before it is once again in direct sunlight
The flowers have nearly had their space

With another skyward glance, I notice new growth

An ancient oak - hundreds of years old
Adorned with bright green, sap-filled luscious new leaves

Each year tree magic creates life anew
This annual juxtaposition of ancient and modern
As fresh new leaves burst forth
From buds brewed in the long dark of winter

14th May

Night Song

Bluebells* at dusk are a real, special treat
They're a sight for sore eyes lying spread at my feet
The song of the blackbirds as loud as the dawn
Heralds the night in, it sounds so forlorn
The sadness that each day has come to an end
Is marked by their chirping
What message it sends?
Are they calling home loved ones, their babes to the nest?
Or marking their territory - hope it holds fast!
Why sing as the night comes?
Perhaps there's no choice
It seems as light changes they have to give voice

16th May

Botanical notes:

Four-lobed blue flowers - germander speedwell I believe
Tall furry trumpet flowers with purple heads
Yellow, white and blue/purple predominate
Field maple and hazel are filling out the mid-level
Nettles abound
Muddle and tangle of greens
Top canopy beginning to fill out as ash leaves sprout
Mum and baby Muntjac deer just strolled by

---

* On learning that bluebells sleep, I went to the Woods at dusk to see for myself

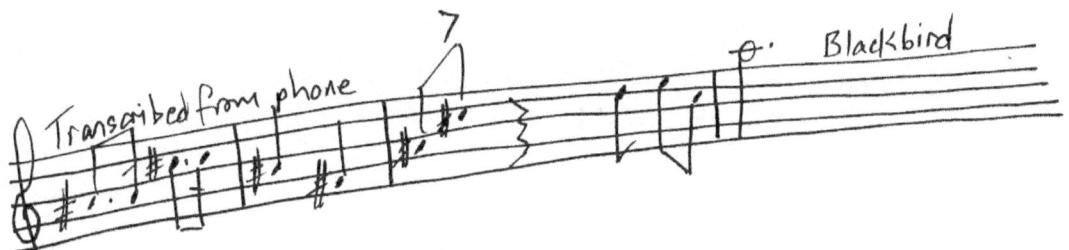

18th May
Dinosaur

A tumble of tangled tresses took my eye for a moment
Then at Seven Oak Corner
A huge dinosaur thrust its limbs towards me
The topmost branch of the oldest oak
The one with the widest girth
Had crashed to the ground
Torn flesh screaming skywards

20th May

Tent 1

A flash of purple caught my eye
Too big for a patch of flowers
Was it perhaps the jacket of another woodland walker?
But as the undergrowth, which had occluded my view, cleared
I saw it for what it was
A tent
A home
The bogeyman!
The homeless

Yesterday's conversation with a Pagan Prison Chaplain came to mind
Apparently, upon their release ex-criminals are given a tent
Offending is seasonal

So am I right to be cautious as I wander these woods?

The world is upside down

This is a beautiful place to live
If I had a choice I would
Many of us will soon find a place to lie upon the earth
Frequent our favourite festival
Go wild for the weekend
The luxury of choice

But in my mind's eye I see other vast rows of tents
Refugees with no place to go
No option but canvas
Edited out of TV coverage
Scandalous
Shut your eyes tight and it will go away

But no! It won't
The world is on the move
And someone has found a home in Kingswood

22nd May
Tent 2

A shared Sunday session
Foraging with a friend for sorrel, plantain, nettle and cleavers
Started from Southbrook
I was the route finder leading the way to the sorrel
On the way to the bluebells
On the track by the Elephant Tree
Or the patch of plantain near Lola's crossroads

And there on the corner was a pink tent
Right next to Colyers Avenue
On the grass verge by the park

Curious to check if it was the one I'd seen in the Woods a few days before
I wandered via the glade
Sure enough - the tent was gone

Should I rewrite my homeless poem, Tent 1?
Such a distinct colour - pinky purple
My foraging companion wondered aloud
"Did it belong to some girls whose parents had let them camp out?"
(In this pink-is-for-girls obsessed world
Gender colour coding dictated that this must be a girl's tent)

And suddenly that was the reality I wanted to prevail
Vivid recollection of Swallows and Amazons
A favourite childhood story
Children camping out on an island reached by a sailboat
A time of innocence and adventure
When it was still possible to drink the water out of the lake

Things are not necessarily what they seem
I will never know
A homeless ex-convict released from jail
Having chosen a glade in Kingswood as temporary lodgings?

Or a couple of girls having a great adventure
Camping out in their own jungle?

23rd May
Fallen

A tumble of tangled tresses takes my eye for a moment,
But it is the smell that tells the story of the great fallen oak
A smell so strong and pungent it stops me in my tracks
I glance down to see which spring flowers are so deeply perfumed
Nothing but mud and the usual verge grasses

A strange feeling of being watched turns me to the right
And staring back at me is the huge eye of a rhinoceros
Recently fallen
A massive limb has ripped itself from the largest of the seven oaks
And the smell is hundred-year-old sap

It smells like time itself

The gash, the wound, is raw and fresh
Sharp edges screaming to the sky
Oozing tree-blood
Redolent with the knowledge of the inner workings of the tree
Centuries of inner life now open to the elements

I realise that there are several trees laying down their limbs
What was vertical now horizontal
Shape-shifting from tree to rhinoceros

Is it age? Weather? Infirmity?
I query how so much life remains in these fallen logs
Still blooming year after year
They live on
What does it take to stop a tree from growing?
They say a tree takes as long to die as it has lived
Chronology encoded in each branch, twig, bud, blossom, fruit and leaf
Two hundred years hence
Long after I have gone
Its heart will live on

8th June
*The Insects Prevail**

Occlusion
The canopy overhead is now closed
Light filters through with difficulty
The dappling on the swamp is dazzling
An iridescence rarely seen
And so many greens
One word seems inadequate to describe this variety
Hold for a moment in your mind's eye
A dandelion leaf, an oak leaf, moss, fern, hazel, briar, grass, algae
What colour are they?

"Green"
We say

I feel obliterated by summer growth
The sheer profusion of summer exhausts me
The tangle of it all
The lack of clear lines
The battle for space
The throng, the reaching
It speaks to my soul
Of my need for space

Perhaps that is why I yearn for the sparse etched lines of a winter landscape
Or the beginning
The hope inherent in the thrust and burst of buds and blooms in spring
Each single flower discernible and identifiable as it emerges

The woodland is different each time I enter
In the sweltering heat of this June afternoon
I wear wellies

---

*Written in Oak Dell

Last night's torrential thunderstorm
Has reduced the forest floor to slippery mud
And I apply all my years of mud-skating to staying upright

Today the most prevalent and busy beings I see are the insects
I have no names for the large black ant-like tree beetle
Scurrying up the trunk where I lean my back
Or the tiny golden grasshopper
Walking around the perimeter of my book as I write
The woodlouse steadily traversing the tree root is the only one I can name
Now is the time of insects
To my right tiny black bugs creep across a leaf
All intent on getting somewhere

There is a different sense of purpose to each season
Like the scurrying squirrels of autumn
Busy stashing their winter food

But today amidst the languor of an overgrown green paradise
A spider abseils from leaf to leaf on a self-spun silken zip-wire
A hornet buzzes towards its nest
And a troupe of mosquitoes dance and zoom
Exquisite patterns in the air

The insects prevail

15th June
On Dog Walkers

A determined breed these dog walkers
As I gingerly paddle my way into the Woods
In the wake of more torrential rain
A small woman in her forties approaches talking on her phone
She is walking a large black dog

Expecting us to meet at the apex of the paths
And to no doubt discuss the lethal terrain underfoot
I am taken aback
She is wearing thin pale pink straw-soled slip-on shoes
She is also deep in conversation
"He drinks water now though. He didn't used to like it"
Is she talking about the dog?
"Yes! The Irn Bru"
And in an instant I realise that the water-drinker is a person

Up ahead I notice a slight man in a grey coat
I am taken by his uneven gait
He is walking a Jack Russell
"Crazy weather" I offer as an opener
"You still need your overcoat" he replies
And we are off
His life story pours out with only the odd prompt from me
His accent tells me he is Irish - from the North
I enquire
He tells of "the troubles" which caused him to leave home
He chose Corby forty-five years ago

Is Kingswood his regular dog walking route?
This isn't his dog it is his daughter's
His dogs, Ben and Paddy, a year and five years dead
Had been Shitzus bought from Gartree Prison

We discuss the sadness of losing a beloved pet
The loss of his own parents
His talented dancing Irish granddaughter
"Tenth in the world" he proudly announces to me and the trees
Which light up with a stray beam of sunlight
It matches the smile on his incredibly smooth skin
"She could have been the best
Had not "the appendix" caused her to cancel a trip to the finals in Canada"

We mention various Irish dance schools
"Costello?"
"No Clifford"
The other names - Cyril Curran, the Nortons
Reminding me how interwoven the Irish are into the fabric of Corby

"What music reminds you of home?" I ask
Bringing forth a litany of singers - "all dead now"
He concludes with Foster and Allan at the Civic, the Willows, the Cube
A man about my own age who remembers my Corby of old!

At the crossroads we part
I am introduced to the dog - Buster Cribben
And I walk away
Enriched by his story
And honoured to have been included even briefly
Into the dog walker's secret club

16th June

The Glow Worm

Last night I saw a miracle
Just lying in the grass
The brightest green I'd ever seen
I couldn't walk on past
I squatted down to have a look
I thought I'd found a fairy
A piece of alien kryptonite
A ring dropped in a hurry
I took a leaf and carefully
I picked it up to see
And on my palm
A glow worm
Was staring back at me
How marvellous is nature that such a thing exists
Emblazoned on my inner eye that emerald light persists

18th June

Footprints

Footprints testify to the presence of other welly-waders
Those who have braved the quagmire before me

The Woods feels exhausted
Gorged
Belly distended with too much water

Something went wrong with the old adage
"Oak before the Ash, there will be a splash
Ash before the Oak we will get a soak"
This has been an unremitting soak

Again the Woods has changed
Canopy cover complete
It is almost dark
Determined fingers of light penetrate the thick cover from time to time
Highlighting the tangle of overgrown undergrowth
Six foot high nettles and granny's porridge* dwarf me

It feels out of balance to me
Almost force-fed

As the canopy has closed - the middle layer bends over
And everywhere I see arches
In contrast I pass some totally straight hazel and dog rose
A little patch of space where I can reach for the sky

I notice again the busy insects
And watch a bee do its work on some white blossom
I am pulled off-course by what I think is a new track
Only to find it is the top path to the swamp
I ponder on the wood's ability to appear new to me each day
An inexhaustible treasure trove

---

*Granny's porridge is my childhood name for cow parsley

July

7th July
Woodland Deprivation Syndrome

For two weeks my twisted knee has kept me housebound
I last entered the Woods at dawn on the longest day
Slipsliding through liquid earth trying to find purchase
As I took one slow painful step after another

Never had it been so wet

The morning chorus was a true delight
Raucous cacophony of sheer being
But right now my heart yearns for the dark
For the stars
For the trees
So I slowly hobble to the woods

Midnight approaching not a soul to be seen
Anticipation is keen
An almost visceral longing

My feet know the way
A night-owl I come alive at night
I have no fear of the dark
I entrust my vision to the soles of my feet
And their sensors come alive

But tonight this dark is absolute
And the undergrowth and foliage so abundant that I cannot see the entrance
Stepping into the blackness on the grass verge
I sense an opening and move through the curtain of leaves

Immediately enwrapped
I take a few steps forward and then stop

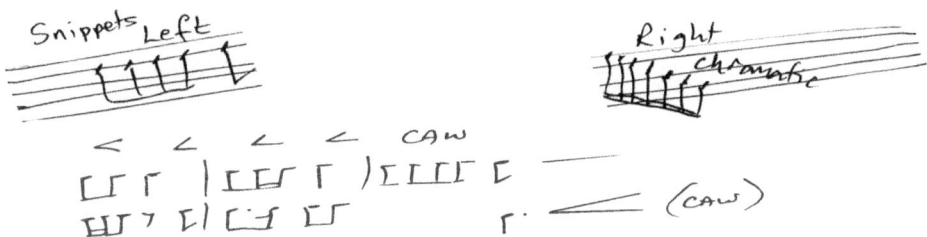

It is like stepping into Narnia

A few short yards separate the bright intrusive street lamps
From this tunnel of trees

My eyes adjust quickly
I stand stock still and allow myself to merge
To become one with the beings of the wood

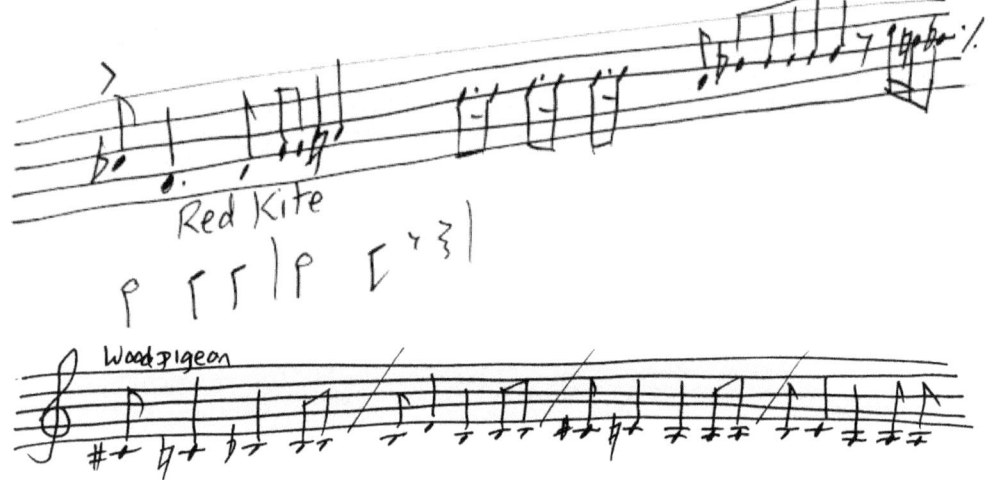

8th August
Goodbye to the Woods

I say goodbye to the Woods
Impenetrable fortress of green
As I leave for my summer travels

Close your eyes and listen
Can you hear the sound of the woods?

The rhythmic wood pigeon call
The call of the kite
The screechy owls passing the relay call from tree to tree
The wind in the trees
Chirping insects

*Open your eyes and look around
What do you see?*

Write your own poem here:

13th September
End of Summer

The Woods is tired and weary
Ready for a rest
Tattered leaves and evidence of a summer full of people

I sit briefly amongst the dry white stalks of spring bluebells
It looks messy
Worn
Needs to return to the earth to encourage new growth

But all is still green
An in-between confused part of the year
The change not yet begun

Blackberries ripe for the plucking tantalise
Red berries appear on the hawthorns
There is a dry and dusty feel to the end of summer
Mushrooms are beginning to emerge amongst the nibbled greenery
But there is still peace to be had
In the shade of an old moss-covered fallen trunk

20th September
Autumn Glimpse

Drops of gold shine out amongst uniform green
Gossamer threads brush my face
As deeper in the woods hazel and hawthorn begin their change
I see a leaf divided in two - half green and half gold

22nd September
Stewardship

Pools of dappled sunlight beckon as I pass
A moment's peace amongst the hurly-burly humdrum have-tos
I step inside

Immediately I am part of an entire ecosystem
As necessary as each leaf but unsure of my part in the order of things

My being does not feed the trees
My footsteps erode the earth
But is my witness not a part of the wheel of life?

Unlike the oak I am not home to hundreds of insects
But I tread lightly on my journey
Behold
Breathe with the trees
Is not my touch a part of nature too?

Alive to the beauty which surrounds me here
I become part of the web
Reaching my energy roots deep into the soil
Drawing strength each day
I am fed from this vast underground web

And in return?
I do what I can to preserve and protect
To prevent destruction
Take stewardship seriously

26th September
Autumn Nights

My feet find their way to my secret entrance
And I step into Narnia

Autumn dark enwraps me

I stand stock still and allow myself to merge
To become one with the beings of the woods

Carefully I move along the tunnel
Long before anything obstructs my way
My aura meets it, measures it, appraises it

Senses on night alert I stand still as the trees and listen

Soughing and swooshing above me
Rising and falling
< >
Wave-like swelling, retreating
I lose myself in the rustling sound
Imagine waterfalls all around

And then I hear the steady tread of approaching footsteps
What to do?
I wrap my black night jacket closely around me and take one step to the side
Obscured from view I disappear myself
Invisibility cloak

But I sense the footsteps are not alone
A walker would pass by without noticing me
But a dog? - that is another question
And as the white beast appears ahead of its owner
I decide to speak out

"I am here" I say "without a dog"
Nervous response followed by quickening, rapidly retreating footsteps

They say you never know who you'll meet in the woods
Indeed
I am the wild woman of the woods that you were all warned about

Alone again I scan widely
All mine - for now
I choose Seven Oak Walk
A fabulous ghost-like shape appears
The damaged oak

Imagining leading a night walk here, I move on
Inhaling the scent of wet pine as I reach the clearing
The light in my mind's eye is so bright I can see the way
Yet as I emerge onto the roadway I am nearly blinded by street lamps

27th September

Tortoise Pace

I approach with excitement and anticipation
Like greeting a lover after a long absence
My feet lead the way as they did last night
The entryway nearly overgrown
I meet slippy mud and bike tracks

As soon as I step across the threshold
An unbelievable sense of wellbeing overcomes me

It truly is a portal

I am dappled with sunlight filtered through a tall waving ash tree
The scent of honeysuckle leads my eyes to some blossoms
Right there at the entrance
I stand smiling as I write
Nettles taller than me add their bitter-sweet tang to the smell
As they reach out with the brambles to greet me

How come I was neither stung nor scratched in my late-night wandering?
Granny's porridge-heads* as big as fists thrust upwards
Everywhere now fully clothed
Leaf patterns harmoniously dancing together
Tall tops of slender ash wave in the wind far above my head
Mud-mush covers the path

How come I hadn't slipped on my night walk?**
The full green crown-cover which had blacked out the stars at night
Now throws a dead trunk into sharp relief
I see the fallen branch over which I stepped last night
My night senses alert to obstacles

I sit awhile on the big log
In a patch of shimmering leaf-filtered sunlight
Barely twenty yards into this liquid green sensory splendour
Vibrant, buzzing, teeming with life force

---

*Granny's porridge is my childhood name for cow parsley

**This poem references the night walk on 26th September

Hawthorn tickles my cheek as I fill myself up with delicious peace
Drink in the sights and sounds and smells
My hands tingle as I feel the energy rising through my body
Indescribable feeling of connection
My arid soul was parched for green and mud

On reaching the main path at my new snail's pace
One much more in tune with the speed of life in the woods
My eyes well up with tears
Such beauty is hard to contain

The trees have joined overhead creating a glorious tunnel
A canopy of shimmering greens and light
I feel momentarily
As if I have stepped into one of Aunt Emmeline's* oil paintings
The struts and limbs a moving sculpture
Created by dark brown trunks and branches
In all shapes and sizes and textures

An urgent shout from a passing youth - busy on his phone - raises no alarm
He strides past intent on his own business
We estate-dwellers share the Woods happily
In one upward glance I see hazel, ash, pine, oak and hawthorn
He returns - a young woman with him
Two of the many privileged youngsters from this most deprived estate
Who walk to school daily through this paradise

I stand transfixed by the ash leaves
The emblem of the Natural History Museum

---

* My Aunt Emmeline was a painter who LS Lowry described as "a true British Colourist".
  Her tree paintings hung on the living room walls in the family home

At the first turning I see a pile of tree bones
Someone attempting to soak up some of the mud
Create some ground to walk on
Has heaped thick twigs into the earth through which I waded at Solstice
It looks like the carcass of an animal picked clean by vultures
The view to the left is dominated by a soaring pine
Such a different green against the others

The rustling of the trees, shushing and sighing
Fills my ears and drowns out the traffic
This tortoise pace makes me present
In a way that no amount of meditation ever achieved
Did I twist my knee to slow me down to the here and now
The what-is
Not the what-will-be?
To do or to be, an age-old personal battle

I plant my roots deep each morning - but then I move
This massive oak has stood right here for over a hundred years
I lean against the thick cushioned trunk
Home to thousands of insects
The view from here is different
Now I see bark patterns clearly on the trees opposite and notice relative girth
This tree was here when the first World War was happening
It was probably as thin as some of the new growth opposite
It knew my father who also used to walk these paths

The wind is getting up
I resolve to make it as far as the glade and pick up my pace slightly
I move through a cloud of dancing aerial ballerinas
Notice where the rich dark loam has been churned by a motorbike
I am dwarfed by the three trunks of the old oaks
Which guard Lola's crossroads

Their flat surfaces act as projection screens for the sun's shadow play
I gaze at the churned-up track
Impassable for all but the bikers who have clearly been enjoying the mud

Just beyond, the sky is visible
Bright hot sunlight busy drying a small section of the path
One area which has survived the rainfall due to this daily drying out session

A dog walker approaches as I hear two feet
Clinking of leads
Panting dogs and eight paws

I reach the clearing
It has not been cut back
And I find myself in a meadow of shoulder-high fluttering grasses

Someone has made a swing on the old oak and I pause to rest
The swing twizzles me round
Affording me a wonderful 360 degree panorama
I am inside a cyclorama and I move as the trees do
Back and forth
Transported to those carefree days of childhood by playing on the swing
I head home refreshed, restored and revitalised
Asking myself once again - who needs a garden?

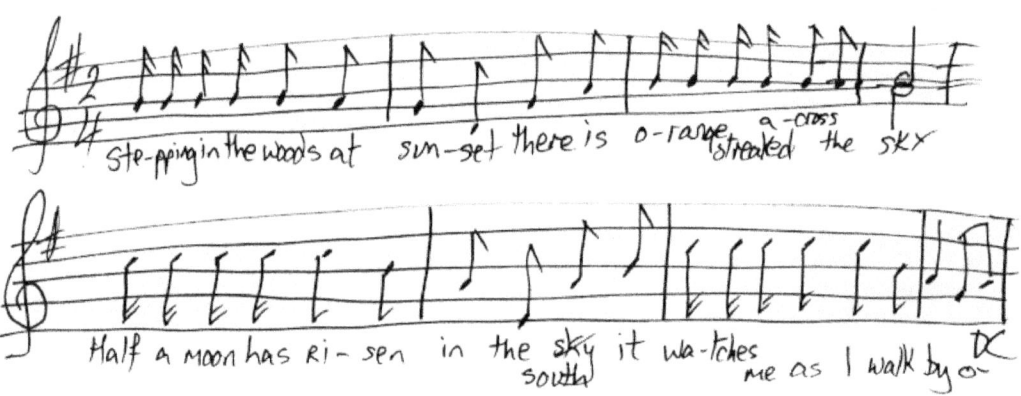

28th September
Fecund

The fecund earth is bountiful this year

Fecund
What an unfortunate word
Hard - with edges - and ugly consonants

We need a word which promises beauty as it emerges from your lips
Tastes tangy
Wrapping your tongue around it should be a joy
Akin to the shock of sweetness of the first blackberry of the year

The sound of this word is harsh, masculine, like a tool
Not right for the springy moss
Or the squidgy mushrooms
Or the proliferation that is nature's harvest

We need a buoyant word
A light and airy, floaty full of water spark of fire word
That tells of the mud, the loam, the humus
The elements from which all life is born

The *"season of mellow fruitfulness"* is upon us
Everywhere berries burst from the trees
Foragers feast
Elderberries have been and gone
But there are still blackberries for the taking
Some not yet ripe

And fruits hang heavy on the boughs
The thunderous sound of apple-fall when a tree is shaken
Unmistakable

Promising weeks of apple pie, stewed apples
Baked apples with cinnamon and raisins
Apple juice and cider

4th October
The Sky is Falling

Today the sky fell on my head
*"So I am off to see the King, Chicken Licken"**
In 59 years of wandering beneath trees
This is the first time I have been hit by an acorn

Autumn usually sees leaves change colour then fall
First the turning then the falling
But this high wind has caused the reverse

Squirrels busy squirrelling away the falling nuts for the coming winter
Golden highlights in the canopy above becoming more obvious
A familiar copper sheen glints up at me
From amongst the years-old leaf debris
The ailing chestnut tree has produced a bumper crop of beautiful conkers
(Perhaps a survival response from a diseased tree)
This is my time to indulge in joyous collecting
Gathering conkers
To make art from nature's bounty

---

*Chicken Licken was a book by SC Licken which I read as a child in which a chicken is hit on the head by a falling acorn and thinks the sky has fallen on his head. He goes off to see the King to complain and meets Turkey Lurkey, Foxy Loxy and lots of other animals along the way

5th October
Coppice

A flash of white birch bark catches my eye and pulls me in to explore
A recently cleared glade
Coppicing makes space for sure though it looks like needless destruction
I struggle with the apparent devastation - but see how nature recovers
Look what is revealed

Fast growing straggly hazel the frontrunner of trees yet to come
Patches of old, old moss
Spreading sorrel on soggy clay loam
Piles of neatly chain-sawed lengths of trees which had met their doom
Lying higgledy-piggledy where they had been felled

Except for some cut trunks of silver birch
(There are very few in Kingswood)
Laid parallel to create a seating square

I sit awhile as the pungent odour of decay assails my nostrils
And slowly survey the cleared space
Imagine a year from now
A whole new universe will exist
For now I throw my head back and count the ash and oak
Forming the circle of swaying treetops
Which surround this new space
This potential
This possibility

6th October
Dog Tree

The two trunks of the tree form a V shape in the sky
Joined at the base they had grown together for a while
Before going their separate ways
Same but different like twins

Someone sprayed graffiti on this special tree
I notice it every time I pass with sinking heart
Saddened by such desecration

Then one day I visited the woods with twins Jack and Oakley
And their nana Jackie

They recognised and greeted this special tree as they passed
They'd always called it their twin tree

On our return however Jack called it the dog tree
Where I had seen graffiti he saw a dog
And my view was transformed forever

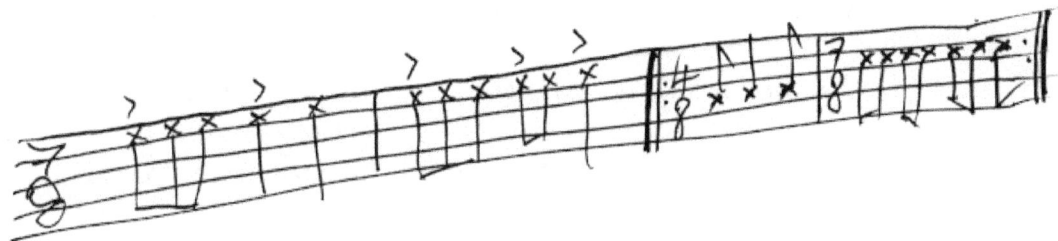

7th October
A Haunt of Peace

The turkey oak is the frontrunner in this year's race to change
Gold is dripping from the sky - so it seems
I stand riveted by this magnificent tree
Pondering the direction of colour change
Top down or bottom up?
I am reminded of a half-painted tree in spring
Changing colour from east to west

Amid the end-of-summer fading green
Some determined new hazel growth
Stands out in its vivid spring-green finery

A pregnant pause
An in-breath
Before the long slow exhalation into hibernation
Nothing moves

I go deeper
Join with the sense of waiting and isness
Without the wind a wonderful enveloping stillness overcomes the place
Further on, having walked along the main artery of this beating heart
Pulsing in unison, breathing together
I am struck by an old gnarled wizened moss-covered tree
I have never previously noticed
An ancient fallen log bids me sit awhile and I begin to see afresh

To ponder shape, form, colour, texture, pattern, light and shade
The preserve of the visual artist
This nature-looking enriches my visual literacy
I practise my visual scales
Here in my own outdoor gallery
Exhibition constantly changing

Dropping my shoulders
I breathe out
Sink deeper
Let go
Enter the "haunt of peace"

My return journey is as if I am in another wood all together

I go forth strengthened and renewed

"Lonely woods with paths dim and silent
A haunt of peace for weary-hearted
There is healing in your shade and in your stillness balm
All those who seek repose from the world's strife and clamour
Find a haven calm and secure and go forth strengthened and renewed" *

---

*Childhood song by Jean-Baptiste de Lully learned in junior school

9th October
The World Turned Upside Down

On stepping into the Woods again
I am immediately connected to the entire forest
Turned on its head
There would be a vast network of roots up in the sky
Anastomosis*, veins, arteries, capillaries, alveoli, nerves
Nature knows how to connect
The trees are linked
Do the roots go underneath the road?
Beneath the tarmac
Do the roots connect with the wild trees on the corner of Alberta Close
Which once were part of the Woods before the estate was built?
They do

---

*Anastomosis: a cross-connection between adjacent channels, tubes, fibres, or other parts of a network

17th October
Colour Box

Copper-tipped turkey oak shedding acorns
Crispy curling ash leaves shrivel drop and scrunch
Stunning autumnal palette transforms the surroundings
Alchemy of green to gold
Blood dripping
Paint-box fiesta

22nd October
Artists

My outdoor studio - Kingswood - is teeming with artists today!
On the way for my daily visit
I come across a long straggling line of them
Intent on drawing the Woods
As I am on writing the Woods
And singing the Woods
A lovely moment of collision

26th October
Going Bald

Showers of golden leaves rain from the trees
Fluttering effortlessly
The trees are slowly stripped of colour
Going bald on top first

30th October
*Abscission**

Perhaps it was a race to beat the coming of the dark
A wish to fall to earth whilst they could still see their way
Or perhaps it was simply time

Without a breath of wind the leaves dropped to the ground
Prolific shedding
A beautifully choreographed snowfall of golden petals

What governs the moment of letting go?
This graceful surrender to gravity

Time to lie down
Return to the earth
Weary of hanging on
Clinging by a spider thread
Abscission - a beautiful word
Somewhere between abseil, decision and precision
Is this the leaf's purpose?
To become food for the tree
A clear defining moment

Do they choose to fly together in a cluster?
Now - let's go - it's our time

---

*Abscission: the natural detachment of parts of a plant, typically dead leaves and ripe fruit

2nd November

Room to Breathe

A bare ash tree with only keys remaining
Greets me as I enter the green and gold tunnel
Acorns littering the forest floor make it difficult to walk
The fall is now in full swing
Bushes and shrubs lining the path are shedding from below
A scant covering of yellowing leaves provides the mid-level perspective
Ankle-deep in toffee-coloured oak leaves
I catch the glint of sunlight on the uppermost branches
This time next week it will already be dark as the year gallops to a close
But for now the glittering golden highlights deceive

The colour palette of this oak/ash/hazel wood
Though beautiful
Is missing the glorious cherry and maple red of the roadside trees

Acorns fall like rain
In the glade, six-foot high dead stalks dominate
Brown, scrunchy and withered
Here several trees have shed from bottom up
Only a few sparse leaves cling on
Patches of hawthorn add a different hue
Fallen ash leaves line the path
Each one a stencil of the Natural History Museum emblem
The chestnut tree stands
Midst a rich comfy carpet of deep orange leaf-fall
A sudden burst of red as I pass a patch of bramble
Picked clean of all but the hardest berries

Tall willowy ash beckon me
Some would say thin and spindly compared to the mighty oaks
But these are the young trees
Making their mark with *"room to breathe"**

---

*The marketing slogan used to persuade Londoners to move to Corby

18th November
Who's First?

Hazel
Lolling lime-green tongues flapping in the wind take the stage
Dominating the mid-canopy
Newly coppiced hazel growth
Still busy growing
Getting as much sunlight as it can before hibernating for the winter
Now that the upper canopy is all but clear
There is a chance to soak up some rays and put in a last growth spurt

Ash
Late to blossom, early to fall
Ash have the shortest season
Their tall straight trunks the scaffolding for the forest

Oak
Tenacious oaks
Stand fully clad
Their full magnificent rust-orange clusters
Proclaim their place at the top of the pecking order
Each individually on display

The turkey oaks with their prickly furry buds
A much brighter yellowy orange
Denuded of their acorns and much leaf-fall
Stand out in a different way

"The change, then the fall", sing the oaks
"When we are good and ready - if at all"

19th November
Tinsel

The ash have cleared the skyline
Dropped their crinkly curled leaves
To show their bones to the sky
The skeleton of the woods is beginning to show

In stark contrast, an ancient oak
Still thick with the lush green foliage of summer
Shows not one hint of change

Yet all around is yellow
Not bright sunlight yellow
But a warming hot-chocolate-woolly-hats-thick-scarves kind of yellow

Spiky turkey oak, devoid of acorns, a bright rich yellow
My glade oak - still green
Seems blissfully unaware that her dress is so last season

As I approach Seven Oak Corner
The grandeur of the oak boughs and trunks
Takes my breath

Here too they hold their leaves
A reminder that despite the nip of frost
We are only half way through autumn
The green of pine and bramble is at odds with the general tone
Except for one orange conifer adding its shocking colour to the mix
Draping and dropping soft needles round a field maple
Like tinsel
Woodland tinsel

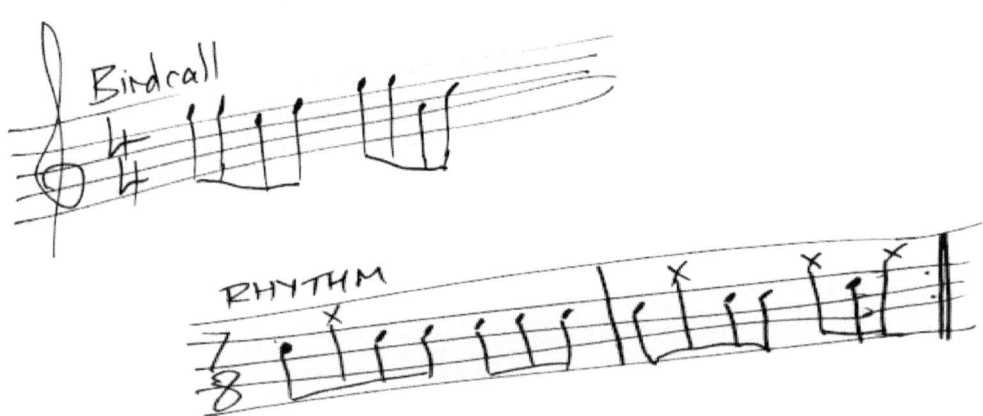

20th November
Treetop Land

That nip of frost in the air had me reaching for a warmer jacket
As the morning call to head for the Woods took hold
The oaks now turning the vista a russet browny gold in concert
Stark ash skeletons hung with bunches of keys
Naked whilst others are fully clad

The oaks have been biding their time
Birch tree reveals dangly catkins

I wonder why some ash have bunches of keys and others don't?
Why some lose their leaves still green
Whilst others are shrivelled and brown?
I later discover that ash, like humans, are dimorphic
Female and male trees differ

The acorn layer at the entrance to the Woods
Is even thicker underfoot
I stoop and collect them in handfuls right there by my feet
Fill my pockets with nature's bounty
Intent on exploring acorn coffee
Unbelievable abundance

Sideways slats of sunlight pick out a wise old face in the thick oak trunk
The birdsong is different now
A squirrel leisurely hops across the track
Winter store cupboard no doubt full to the brim
I realise that the bare branches allow me to see birds previously hidden
By lush summer growth
I see a bird and a squirrel way up high
One tip-tapping the branch
The other, bushy tailed, busy getting ready to fly to the next tree

We landlubbers are so limited in our movements

The aerial ballet amongst the treetops is truly impressive
Looping the loop, darting through trunks and branches
Have I never looked up before?
I feel as though I have stumbled upon a secret world
Treetop Land
Up the "magic faraway tree"*

Caw caw caw
I hear a snippet of Dvorak's seventh symphony

A startled wood pigeon takes flight
Flap flap flapping noisily away

Another bird leaps into the unknown gliding upon invisible air currents
"Cheep cheep"
Birds really do say cheep cheep

With a thud
A sizeable clump of leaves and acorns
Plummets heavily to the ground behind me
No graceful floating leaf
This was a weighted drop

Scrat scrat scratting close by alerts me to hopping birds
Foraging in the leaf-fall

I pause at the crossroads
My shadow large and clear telling me that it is noon

Looking north I see that the trees have been stripped from above
Meeting the tree line of the still burgeoning hazel copse

---

*Enid Blyton's book "The Magic Faraway Tree" was an all-time favourite book as a child

Jubilant dog walker approaches - Patty, barmaid at the Labour Club
We excitedly swap autumn sightings
As her dog rummages in the undergrowth
She tells of a deer seen a few days ago

Distant barking warns of squabbling dogs
And I head for home
Leaving the lunchtime woods free for the canine club

And for the huffing puffing runners out in their woods for a midday jog

Unbelievably I find yet another new unexplored track
And leave this magic forest that just keeps on giving

21st November

Impressions

The pull of the Woods on this clear blue autumn morning proves irresistible
Bargaining with my schedule to free up time I step inside
Wind through trees
Traffic
Birds in surround sound
A held expectancy
A breath at the top of the cycle
Before the long slow letting go
Into leaf-fall and the slumber of winter
But for now
The Woods is alive
With the sound of an Indian-summer day

23rd November

From Above

Gazing into the dying fire
I see glittering jewels and faces in the embers

Trance-like I leave my body and fly free in my mind
Looking down I see the view from above
The pathways through the woods
Outlined in Aboriginal pointillist perspective

The glow of the fire now the bright eye of a dragon
The tree tops the lumps and bumps of its scaly back

26th November
Tree Orchestra

Walking through the wet dripping woodland as night draws in
I feel deeply connected
Bare branches vividly etched against the rapidly darkening sky
End-points of a vast underground network
Each time I send my imaginary roots down into the soil
I become part of it
Anastomosis
Mushrooms and toadstools are part of it too
The visible part
But beneath the surface their fibres intertwine
Weaving a web of immense proportions

Each person who joins my orchestra
Represents a tree
There will be sixty musicians
One for each year of my life
Woven together through community connections
Into a human web
Just as intricate and vital as the trees and mushrooms

28th November
Late Autumn 1

Three weeks of autumn left
Determined oaks drink up every last ray of the weakening sunlight
Fat orange leaves almost bursting

A passing child inquires of his Irish grandma
"Don't leaves fall off the trees in autumn?"
She tells him that the seasons have changed
"The colours are more vivid" she says
A much yellower autumn than usual
Due to "the climate change"

The floor carpet is now pale green as the hazels finally succumb
The acorns are gone
Either gathered by squirrels
Or trodden into the damp earth by passing walkers

Tree trunks covered with white lichen
Paintball-style
Are beginning to predominate
As the rest of the wood settles down

My bluebell glade
Is now a series of horizontal broken-off branches
And tall reaching trunks
Woodland skeleton laid bare

Birds of three weeks ago are quiet now
Have they flown away to warmer climes?

I sense a noticeable intake of breath
A pause

A ferocious wind would put an end to this liminal waiting
And clear the trees
Signalling autumn's end

But one or two resolute oaks are still summer-green
With just a hint of autumn-yellow
I wonder
Who is the conductor of this seasonal symphony?
Who knows the score and understands the chronology of leaf-fall?

29th November

Late Autumn 2

Special scrunchy sound as I brush past a beech hedge
Tastily hung with toffee-coloured leaves

Twenty-one toadstools standing guard just inside the woods

A busily scampering squirrel

Beautiful frost on grass in the centre glade

Some oak leaves have decided today is their day
Not a breath of wind
But they lazily float to earth

As I walk a squirrel leaps from treetop to treetop
Keeping pace with my determined tread
A magpie's fat white belly flashes above me
Its drilling call ricochets around me
Another falling leaf?
No - a darting robin

December

2nd December

Betwixt and Between

I sit on my moss-covered throne and ponder the crossroads
Which way to turn? Left, right, straight on?
At every juncture we make decisions

Not a breath of wind

In front of me a few straggling hazel tongues - now very sparse
Opposite, stand graceful tall spindly trunks of young ash
To my right a wonderful entanglement catches my eye
Nearby I recognise the familiar old gnarled hawthorn

A solitary oak leaf above me decides it's the moment to let go
Adding to the carpet
Deepening by the day now
Keeping the earth warm
Yes the oaks are finally slowly shedding
Their leaves two nights ago were magical
Glittering
Frost-covered

Some orange still adorns the rooftop of the woods
But leaf-fall is almost complete

Only three weeks to go until we step across the threshold of the year

Until the light returns

Another oak leaf takes the plunge but never makes it
Caught on a tangle of interwoven undergrowth and lower branches
It nestles next to a crinkled ash leaf
Destined never to know earth
Permanently sky-bound
Betwixt and between

I move on and take a little-known track past a field maple
Beautiful yellow leaves thinning to rice paper before they drop
I find myself in the Hazel Copse
Old trees branch out in every possible direction
I reach my arms to the heavens
Mimic the line, the thrust, the shout of this multi-branched tree

The track takes me to my Squirrel Glade
From there to the Elephant Tree
A lovely walk
Full of glades and stopping places

3rd December

The Photo Time Machine

Taking a photo of the Bluebell Glade in late autumn
I am reminded of the one I took in spring
Effortlessly transported back
To that time of deep rich blue and dappled sunlight
Through spring-green trees
Intensely grateful for this commission
Which bids me stay a while longer
To really see
To really be
Measuring this gradually changing year
One day at a time
One flower
One bud
One leaf

4th December

Space

Today as I stood barefoot in the fairy ring
Sending my roots deep to join the others
A young man in a purple hoody came along the path

He nodded
Unperturbed
Greeted me with a friendly "y'alright?"
And proceeded to sit on the log
Roll a cigarette
And do something with his phone
Totally unfazed by this white-haired woods-woman
Standing barefoot amongst the mushrooms
Arms reaching to the sky

I - on the other hand
Questioned whether I could continue my most private of rituals
So close to another person

The trunk of the tree which forms part of the ring
Just about obscured him from view
So I continued
Singing into my chakras
And circling my arms around

When he was ready he simply left

Intent as I was on inner affirmations
With eyes gently closed
I heard him go
A slow tread on scrunchy newly fallen leaves

We give each other space in these woods

As I moved off
I passed a young woman watching her two charming small dogs
Who were nuzzling amongst the leaves
Dog walkers, school children, ramblers
Estate dwellers, young people, joggers
Wildlife Trust workers
We all use this place

I thought I recognised the Wildlife Trust range-rover
Parked up by the first crossroads
But no - it was a young couple taking in the view

As I approached, the driver wound down the window
And apologised
"Hope we're not disturbing you
Just came to roll a joint and look at the view
Isn't it beautiful?"
"Specially when you're tripping" I quipped
They smiled and waved me on

Yes, we give each other space in our woods

5th December
Oak Abscission Day*

Today was the day of the oak divers
Not sea divers you understand
But air divers
Brave parachute jumpers
The slightest breeze gave a nudge to those ready to go for it
Like big brown snowflakes they flutter and fall
Some get waylaid, catching on lower branches
Others get taken by invisible air currents
To a resting place far from home

I watch as leaves from the topmost branches
Bravely decide to leap into the unknown
Sixty, seventy, eighty feet below
I become fixated on velocity
How fast does a falling leaf fall?
One, two, three, four....ten or twelve seconds?
They seem to fall at more or less the same rate
I do the maths
Sixty feet in twelve seconds
A neat sum
Five feet per second
Three hundred feet per minute
One thousand eight hundred feet per hour

A new path brings me to an unknown oak which is shedding merrily
I can't resist - I reach out
Hope to catch a falling leaf and put it in my pocket
Save it for a rainy day
I reach this way and that
Caught in a spontaneous beautiful dance
Choreographed by nature
And the interplay between the decision of each leaf
And the vagaries of wind and air currents

---

*Abscission: the natural detachment of parts of a plant, typically dead leaves and ripe fruit

The leaves come to rest on what appears to be a cork-tiled forest floor
I feel the warmth and thickness of this natural carpet
Insulation, dedication, disintegration

Each leaf has technically left home
Taken leave of its mother
After months of busy photosynthesis
Storing sunlight and water in chloroplasts
Being the "fresh-air makers and stale-air gobblers"*
A totally essential part of the ecosystem
Here they are ready to start out alone

Some leap together, like lemmings
In seemingly random pairings
Briefly, once airborne, they are mobile
But that is short-lived
Once landed they are still again

Then I see the oak leaf goblins
A whole gang, troupe, gaggle of them
Dancing together and running with the pack
Whipped along by the wind like a Victorian child rolling a hoop
These wind-propelled oak leaves
Are the sproinging spring lambs of autumn
The risk-takers

The sky-divers

The last leaves to fall

---

*A play I wrote for Tree Dressing Day one year featured a future world where trees had been replaced by fresh-air makers and stale-air gobblers

7th December

Three Leaves

Wet misty late autumn day
Surely leaf-fall is complete?
I look around
Remnants of residual orange still hold out
Thin covering of tenacious oak leaves
Clinging to the topmost branches
But the bones of the bare trees predominate
Sky now visible everywhere

My fairy ring remains

At the swamp I find a vivid green moss-covered log
Opposite a tumble of fallen branches
I take my usual path through the archway to my oak-glade studio
This tree is in full leaf - but still yellowy green
I wonder how many species of oak live in this wood
Watching odd oak leaves take the plunge
Diving from the top board

Taking yet another unfamiliar track
I find myself in the presence of a mighty oak
Thick massive corrugated cork ridges
I thrill at its powerful aura
It seems naked and male
Ash have female and male trees
Maybe oak do too
The aura reaches a long way and I sense it from afar
Imposing
Potent
There

Past the Dragon Oak back on the main path
I head for my Bluebell Glade
Did I ever take an autumn photo?

Next to the Conker Tree, stunning in its wet nakedness
Stands a green oak
It looks like an interloper
An anachronism
A clothes-wearer at a nudist colony
Strangely out of place

The freshly revealed bare branches
Make endless struts and frameworks all around me
Riveted, I realise what I want for my sixtieth birthday
A much longed-for trip to the Yorkshire Sculpture Park

I take pictures in the stark denuded Bluebell Glade
Marvel at the contrast of the seasons
Capture the lattice work on Stan's Ash Tree
And head for home

Passing a solitary cherry tree I see three leaves
These few remaining lozenges of bright red
Shocking against the black and white background
I am minded of the girl in the red coat
I pocket the tiniest leaf (ever) and take it for three-year-old Sophia
The bigger one for six-year-old sister Eva
The biggest one for Clare their mum

Once upon a time there were three leaves...

14th December
Five Leaves and an Immigrant Dog

Whilst I was sleeping the oak leaves fell
Plunging us into an early winter landscape
It must have only just happened
Since dry light-brown leaves dust the surface of the wet mulch underfoot

I pass one oak tree with nut-brown leaf clusters on its lower branches
They refuse to fall

Not a leaf to be seen on the mighty turkey oaks
Pines now visible through bare crown canopy
I slipslide to my glade to check on the late droppers
And find that everything seems to have caught up
Finally

Red cherry leaves again catch my eye
My path is the same as last week
And though I plunge into the undergrowth at random
I am curiously led to a berry bush
With tiny drops of blood-leaves scattered around it
Vivid against the mud

I select five leaves
Lay them in the palm of my hand
Matruschka doll style

Finding myself on the main path
I check the last oak next to the Conker Tree
Gingerly she has started to peel off her layers of leaves
A spattering of green gold oak leaves
Dots the dark brown chestnut-leaf carpet

As I leave I meet Oscar the dog
And he inspires a fantastic new story idea

"He's from Cyprus you know" proclaims Marjorie his owner
She, like me, is marvelling at the winter beauty of old trees revealed
"He's a survivor
He forages you see
The first nine months of his life he was feral"

I ask why she got a dog from Cyprus

"He's a rescue dog
They let them run wild in Poland and Lithuania and Cyprus
So they end up here
He has a passport
It says Oscar - but I call him Ollie!"

"Does he speak English?" I joke

Delighted at the brand new concept of immigrant dogs
"He has selective language skills" her wry retort
"Efharisto Oscar, parakalou" I say to the dog
Dredging up my tourist Greek
Unperturbed he nuzzles for acorns
And I head for home with a new storyline

19th December
Air, Land or Sea

Sitting on the stump at the crossroads
I notice a squirrel up in the treetops
Tail spread wide yet hardly moving
Tiny thin branches support her weight
As she swings up and down
Trapeze artiste supreme
I creep close - transfixed
But the squirrel is oblivious to my presence
As she sits nibbling the uppermost leaves of a tree I cannot identify
Helicopter keys flutter to the ground
The branches are wispy and drooping
Birch-like but not a birch
She nibbles on unperturbed

Down on the ground I see a dog chasing a squirrel
Here on the floor they are vulnerable

Squirrels scampering across the roof of the woods
Parachutes at the ready
Certainly seem invincible
No yapping snapping dogs giving chase

I ponder the relative safety of air, land or sea

As the autumn draws to a close
All the trees have finally caught up
Even the last dressed oak has shed her leaves
Having kept her autumn cloak until the very end

I imagine the dramatic reveal as she gave it up

"Ta-dah! Of course I knew it was time to bare all
I was just waiting"

This morning I stood barefoot in my fairy ring
But tonight as I leave the woods for my solstice break
And stand with my back against a tree
Peering up at the star-studded almost winter blackness
I wonder what change two weeks will bring

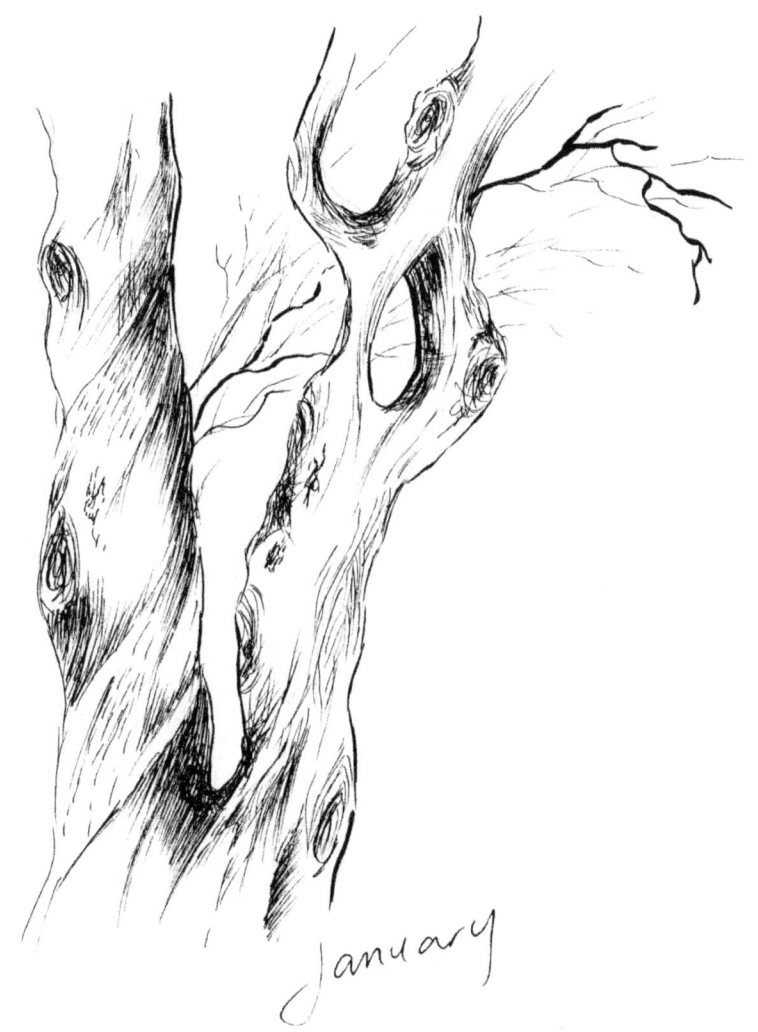

5th January
Winter walk 1

Naked trees
So many skin tones, knobbles, protrusions
Smooth unblemished hazel trunk
Life-worn pitted gnarled old hawthorn
Virile tall straight ribbed oak
Older oak with spiky lumps
Twisty turny bent
Moss-covered
Furry
White-dot splattered
Ivy-patterned
Textured trunks
Ancient
Sproingy soft with age

The chestnut with its darker wood stands out
Here in the Kingswood forest sauna, or nudist beach

15th January
Winter Walk 2

Slowly the mushrooms mulch
Each visit they are disappearing
Gelatinous white mass
Beginning to merge with the dark, dank, wet vegetation

Stunning beauty of the Conker Tree, cast in smelted iron

Undisturbed hazel grove
Straight hazel poles fan out, take space, ready to be useful

I find another new path today leading from Squirrel Glade
There are many now revealed without the overgrowth of undergrowth

Wending my way along it I find myself at the Elephant Tree
I greet it as an old friend then move on to the Monkey Oak

17th January

Bare Trees

There is a starkness to the trees in winter
A bareness which cuts through to the heart of the matter
A strength too
A determination
Nothing to hide behind
There they stand - warts and all
Revealed
"Here we are" they say, nay, proclaim
"We breathe for you"
The bare trees talk to me
In voices loud and clear
"Be strong, be brave, be fearless
Be who you are my dear"

28th January

The Squirrel

A solitary squirrel scurries sleuth-like
Amongst the decaying leaves
Doesn't she know it's winter?
Or is this a mid-hibernation nip to the larder?
She scrit-scrats about, this way and that
"Now where did I leave those nuts?"

8th February
Pathways

On tracks laid bare by lack of foliage
I criss-cross this ancient forest
Clearly not the only meanderer
I marvel at new routes amongst old roots
And find a siamese-twin tree conjoined at heart and womb

9th February
Waiting

The stillness and the sameness of the Woods in winter strike me
An outbreath
Held
Waiting for the thaw
The rising of the sap is slowly, imperceptibly beginning
Catkins hang
Snowdrops peep
Minuscule green buds appear
But for now we wait
On these long, dull, lifeless grey days

Snow keeps trying to fall
But although it is cold, it is not quite cold enough
Only a sprinkling of white on my coat remains

The trees stand strongly and wait
The only movement the dart of winter birds
The scamper of squirrels searching for food

Underground new life is growing in the womb of the earth
But for now we watch as we await Persephone's return

17th February
The Stirring

Quietly, persistently
Life is returning to the seemingly barren woodland
Catkins flutter
Tiny almost imperceptible green tips appear
I touch my third eye to the minuscule bud and feel the stirring

A massive shard of rotten oak blocks my way
My eye is drawn to a round hole in the trunk
The temptation to peek is irresistible

In one glance I can see around and inside
Kingswood through the looking glass
A wide-angle lens view

An ivy-covered tree trunk shimmers in weak sunlight
I move through a quagmire towards the sound of a pair of woodpeckers
Morse code in the distance
The birds heralding imminent spring

27th February
Storm Doris

In search of Storm Doris I enter the woods
I was away when she called
Up North
I saw the trail of havoc her brief visit had caused
As I made my way southwards back to Corby

Broken-off twigs and branches lay like autumn leaves
A great day for wooding
But otherwise Kingswood seems to have fared well
Here she stands
Lazily yawning as the sap stirs her out of her mild winter reverie

March

6th March

Moonstruck

As dusk falls I step into the woods
Wrap myself in the cloak of peace

Lying on the fallen trunk in Oak Dell
I become one with the beautiful night sky
Seen through the lattice weave of intertwining branches

Later I am entranced by the reflection of two trunks in the moonlight
I trace these moon-shadows as they criss-cross the forest floor
Effortlessly I "climb" horizontally to the top of each tree
Follow every twist and turn
My world momentarily flipped topsy-turvy

Incredible shapes are emblazoned on the mud and leaves
Like a child jumping over pavement cracks
I hop squirrel-like from tree to tree
I am led to edges
Deep wet mud and puddles
Compelled to only walk on the shadows

And so I play
A moonstruck woodland sprite

12th March

Peter and the Wolf

At the swamp I find three ducks and "Peter and the Wolf" comes to mind
The birds twitter above
"What kind of a bird are you if you can't fly?" sings the flute bird
"What kind of a bird are you if you can't swim" answers the oboe duck
Both unaware of the approaching clarinet cat
Land? Air? Water?
Which is safest?
Who has the edge in the game of survival?

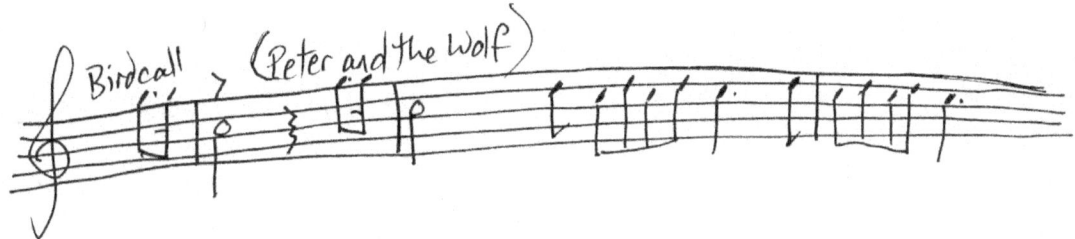

14th March
The Quickening

Violets spill from the grass verge
Grape hyacinths push their way through the green
Turning my window box into a heavenly purply blue
The Woods is still too wet for spring flowers
Primrose Place is ankle deep in water
But Toffee Beech hedge has green tips
And I greet some new buds as I enter the woods

Exploring new pathways at dusk
I revise my assessment of Doris* damage
On my way to the Anemone Patch from Oak Dell
My way is blocked by a recent violent tree-fall
The trunk is split in several places
In its collapse it smashed into several other trees
Devastation
Clambering over it I find a way through
Emerging at Mum's Tree
Only the main path is easily passable

The eventide birdsong has fallen silent
I am wrapped in that special cloak of stillness

Taking the second crossroads
I struggle through the quagmire
Where purple orchids will soon appear
To Bluebell Glade

Hard to believe that this place will soon be filled
With the same heavenly blue of my window box
I sit for a while on a damp mossy log
Sensing where we are in the turn of the seasons

The quickening is here

---
* Storm Doris raged for several days in March 2017

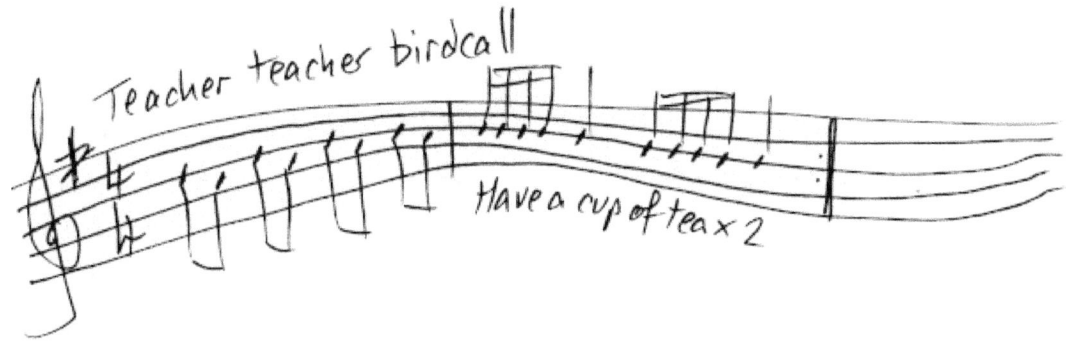

The balmy air
The jacketless walks
The green-tipped hedges and bushes
All point to the coming of spring
Blossoms on some trees already
There is no stopping this and it feels exciting
I reluctantly bid the woods goodnight as I head for home

18th March

Persephone's Return

Stepping inside the woods with Larissa one of the violinists
Eager to show her where we will perform
I am shocked to see how far spring has suddenly sprung

Someone with a giant paint roller
Has walked through the woods
And evenly applied a coat of green paint to mid-level

Overnight what was brown and white
Sparse and bare and patchy
Is covered with green
As more and more buds burst out of their winter coats
And take the stage

White hawthorn blossom and early pink cherry blossom
Tease on the outskirts
But here within
It is the vibrant green of the hedges and bushes which fills me with hope

The next morning I wake early and feel the call
I invite a friend to join me to witness the spring equinox in the woods
The sun obligingly accompanies us as we cross the grass to the woods
Our first treat is the pussy willows covering one tree like a fluffy coat
Big furry buds exquisitely soft to touch adorn this tree
Alone amongst the still-bare oak and ash
I gently touch my third eye to one of the buds
And greet the spring

Turning, we move on towards the entrance
And I see that finally the primroses have managed to emerge
From the sodden waterlogged earth
I bow, as we do at yoga
And so it begins

Namaste I say to the primroses
The grace in me meets the grace in you
I notice some pink primroses
Namaste, new colours I say
Namaste to the yellow celandine
Stars of vibrant buttercup-yellow here on the grass verge
Namaste to the humble days-eye
Namaste I greet the hawthorn blossom
And resolve to continue this practice with each returned friend
Only by knowing our patch do we know what we are losing or gaining

The paths in the woods have dried up a bit
I toy with the idea of leading my guided walk this way to the glade
I watch my friend clambering over fallen trees
Is this do-able with 30 people?
I think not
But arriving at the performing glade via a circuitous route
I realise how excited I am about *Woman of the Woods**

---

*On 2nd April 2017 I led sixty people around the woods as part of the Our Woods project, from Primrose Place to the central glade, where members of my orchestra and four young violin pupils performed the music I had composed alongside these poems. On the way I read a selection of my new writing

8th April
The Bees are Dying

It was the absolute stillness of the bee which gave it away
This was no sleeping beauty
Chest rising and falling
Life causing movement from within
Nor was it a resting bee
Pausing for breath in the middle of a busy day

A gentle nudge with a long stick
Elicited no angry buzz or hasty flight
No - this bee was dead
In the prime of life

What has happened to cause bees to drop from the sky
And lie stock-still on a mossy rotting log in the woods?

O for the hover and drone of bees
Heavy with pollen
Flitting from flower to flower
On a lazy sunlit afternoon

Without their industry
Who will pollinate the plants?
We preside over the end of life as we know it
At our peril

9th April
The Joy of Living
Signs of spring all around

I am greeted this morning by a green tree
Where only yesterday
Bare branches stood stark against the sky across the rooftops

To my utter delight, bluebells appeared
Two days after my Woman of the Woods event
And each day since I have marked their progress
As the undergrowth develops patches of the heavenly blue

The grape hyacinths are going over
I thank them for having held the colour
Celandine too are beginning to fade
But the wood anemones are huge
Speedwell and violets sprinkle the grass
Amongst my patches of proliferating primroses
Dandelions are even ready to blow seeds
And daisies are coming through
Spring nettles, bright chlorophyll green, are everywhere
I wonder what the other green flowers* are amongst the bluebells

Sitting in the Bluebell Glade one day
When I could count them one at a time
I marvelled at how a single stem could appear
Among the leaves of lush foliage
And unfurl hyacinth-like

Further on just past the Dinosaur Tree
Is a log with bluebells, anemones and primroses in view
As I sat there yesterday I saw a dead bee which I honoured with an ode

---

*Dog's mercury

Later a chat with Mushroom John
And a chance encounter with my sister Julie and her beloved dog

I love this place
Our village square
No "forest bathing clubs" needed here

And meanwhile
A whole month early
The cherry blossoms are out on Dunedin Road
Almost too much beauty
But I soak it all up

I see white blossoms
And the deep different blue of the flowers near the crossing
Amazing pale green spring buds on the trees on the way to the pine
The huge chestnut buds, flaccid leaves, developing candles
Magnolia magnificence all around

The richness of nature's beauty
In this joyous time of spring lambs

Free
For all to enjoy
Right here
In Kingswood

Bird Bop from Forest Fragments

Each fragment can be played alone or in any chosen combination in any octave.

About the author

As a playwright and theatre director, Paula has written and staged over fifty plays for Corby Women's Theatre Group and Shout! Youth Theatre. Her play "Women of Steel", which tells the story of Corby through the eyes of women and children, became a book which received critical acclaim as an accurate and accessible living history of a proud former steel town and its people.

In 2016 Paula composed the Sounds of Home Suite, an orchestral work based on interviews with people from over thirty nationalities who had chosen Corby as their home. Last year she was commissioned to write her debut composition for brass bands, Impressions of Barnwell.

This is Paula's first book of poetry.

"Poetry for me acts as a personal emotional camera. This is the first time I have shared such intimate observations with anyone else. May they be your portal into the glorious Kingswood."

About the illustrator

Fanoulla Georgiou studied Fine Art, Practice and Theories at the University of Derby. She has exhibited widely and runs classes and workshops in the local area. Her current focus is bringing creative arts back into schools. In her own creative practice, she is currently working on written word and combining text with image. She particularly enjoys layering words and poetry with photography and mixed media; a way of illustrating layers of thought and experience. Subjects can be anything, from absorbing the essence and atmosphere of a new place, to being quietly pensive in her studio.

Fanoulla is married, with two boys and has been in Corby for ten years, which she proudly calls her home town.

She worked with Paula on the "Inspiring Kingswood" project where they introduced local children from the neighbouring Kingswood Estate to the local woodland.

About the designer

Spider Redgold is an artist and published writer. Currently living in Sydney, her business card says Lesbian Adventuress. She spends her time busy about the tree of life making ceramics, rituals and stirring her cauldron as a lifelong activist for the liberation of women.

About the editor

Antonia Burrows is a teacher and activist who runs a feminist library and community centre.

About the sub editor

Bronwen Evans is an adventurer, teacher, nature lover, gardener, linguist and photographer.

www.ingramcontent.com/pod-product-compliance
Lightning Source LLC
Chambersburg PA
CBHW081415080526
44589CB00016B/2545